Green Furniture: Surprising Facts & 15 Strangely Stylish

Phieby Ibrahim

CONTENTS

ACKNOWLEDGMENTS

Some people obsess over furniture. Others hardly even notice it's there. One way or the other, making environmentally savvy choices in furnishing your home or office can make a big difference in your impact on the planet and your health. The modern sustainability movement has attracted such a large number of innovative designers that it's hard to know where to start. In this article we won't be listing every green furniture company or designer under the sun but rather give a rundown of basic concepts that might guide your search. Of the specific products and brands we do mention, not all will be budget-friendly for everyone--at this point, a lot of the green design is still specialty stuff, and thus pretty high-end. But don't worry. There are always cost effective ways to go green. Keep reading to learn more about the best ways to go green with your furniture.

SUMMARY OF GREEN FURNITURE

Green Furniture Concept makes sustainable seating and acoustic lighting solutions for public indoor areas. ... 'Seamless' means room for more people when needed and the possibility of designing grand furniture configurations in scale with large spaces.

1. WHAT IS GREEN FURNITURE

A bitter truth – the furniture you use at home or office negatively influences the environment. This may not be something you would consider upgrading every not and then. After all, much of your furniture is probably wood – a natural and renewable resource.

Buying green furniture is a way to live an eco-friendly lifestyle. Unfortunately, every single furniture in your home is made from wood, doesn't mean it is green furniture. You need to check it doesn't use toxic materials and is sourced from a sustainable forest.

If you're ignoring this, you're doing as much damage to the planet as mining for coal or drilling for oil. And, this is why you need to understand what green furniture is and why you should use it at home.The base most stolen in a baseball game is second base.

What is Green Furniture

It is not a furniture unit that's painted green!

Any furniture unit that's made in an eco-friendly way, and doesn't cause any harm to human as well as the mother nature is called green furniture. Usually, it is made from FSC Certified Wood, recyclable metal or plastic, and other discarded materials.

Each green furniture unit should also be recycled or repurposed over and over again. Furniture made from natural materials like bamboo and rattan are perfect examples of green furniture.

Wood can also fall into this category but only if it is one of the following types:

Renewable

According to this concept, if you're planting at least one or more trees in return of using a tree for making furniture, it should be termed under green furniture.

Of course, it takes a long time to grow trees but as long as you're planting new trees at the same rate as they are cut down, it will be a renewable resource. Felling of trees must also be taken into consideration along with plantation and growth time of trees.

For example, by the time a manufacturer cuts down trees, they should own more trees of the same age that are ready to be cut down at that time. Of course, it puts an impact on the environment, but it's very limited, plus there is never a shortage of wood.

Even better if more than one tree is planted in place of the one cut down.

Reclaimed

Green furniture can also be used to describe furniture made from wood reclaimed from lakes, rivers, old furniture, houses, barns and warehouses. This wood is already fallen. Using them for making furniture has no or minimal impact on the environmental. Reusing it is just finessing its form to give it some purposeful function.

This type of wood is likely to create an item with a variety of different colors, patterns, and textures. For many, reclaimed wood is a time-worn masterpiece that adds a certain beauty, originality, and story to its surroundings while some others choose it for strength and durability. It may even have different types of wood, making up its construction.

Using furniture made from reclaimed wood can help lower the annual demand for wood. So if you love nature and want to give the old wood a second life, do choose reclaimed wood furniture. Most of the time, reclaimed logs are wider that tell a story. So those wanting to have wider planks of wood can go for reclaimed wood.

Reused

Perhaps one of the most popular ways to acquire green furniture is to simply purchase something that someone else no longer wants.

The environmental impact has already been dealt with; you will simply be prolonging the life of the item by giving it a new home. It is always possible to repaint or varnish the furniture to meet your own taste. Shabby home décor that's one of the most popular home decorating trends is possibly related to reusing old furniture.

You can even pay someone to refurbish it for you, providing you with a piece that looks new but is actually repaired to continue its duty.

Repurposed

If you ever tried to make something useful from unused wood slats that were in pretty good condition, you were possibly contributing to the environment. The theory of repurposing revolves around giving a new function to an unused material.

You can minimize your ecological footprint by furnishing your home with green furniture made from repurposed wood. Making furniture items from pallet wood is a considerably good example of repurposing, but there are certain toxicity issues that need to be taken into account at once.

Aside from material sourcing, the scope of green furniture also expands to furniture made from recycled plastics and metals, but not all of them are green. The ones made in an environmentally-friendly way, with minimal resources and emissions can only be termed under green furniture.

So it very crucial to consider both the production process and material sourcing when purchasing new furniture. Furniture made from renewable wood can also be contributing to carbon footprint if it is not produced in an environmentally-friendly way.

The best way to verify is to check for the designated wood certifications or directly ask the manufacturer; they can surely help you to decide upon a green furniture piece.

If you want to lower your overall impact on the environment, start from limiting your needs and using eco furniture. These steps can surely help us to minimize deforestation as well as its disastrous effects on nature.

It is important to recycle or purchase one piece of green furniture a year. If every household did this, the environment could be rescued in no time.

2. SURPRISING FACTS ABOUT THE ECO-FRIENDLINESS OF FURNITURE RENTAL

A recent WalletHub "2017's Greenest States" study ranked California as one of America's top 15 eco-friendly states. The state also ranked in the top five for "Eco-Friendly Behaviors" and top 15 for "Climate Change Contributions." The two Northwestern states, Oregon and Washington, also ranked highly in "Eco-Friendly Behaviors" and in the top half of states for "Climate Change Contributions."

According to the study, California ranks highly because of the eco-friendly behaviors of its citizens and state government. The state focuses significant resources on green initiatives and is a global leader in innovative climate change programs.

Whether you live in California or anywhere else in the country, you can support eco-friendly efforts of your own to help make a difference. One way is choosing furniture rental for your home furnishing needs. Because of the durability and longevity of quality furniture, a piece of rental furniture is often reused up to six times before being sold in a clearance outlet. In contrast, a piece of furniture purchased new is typically only reused up to three times before polluting a landfill.

Additionally, furniture rental supports eco-friendly initiatives and reduces the carbon footprint of furniture in several other ways.

Reduces Consumer Waste

A 2009 study by the Sustainable Furniture Council showed that 86 percent of furniture buying consumers worry about global warming. As evidenced by the growing popularity of sustainable lifestyle choices, many people actively look for eco-friendly furnishing options. In California, for example, there's significant activism focused on reducing landfill waste from items like low-quality retail furniture.

This waste also concerns Rachel Hulan, ASID, owner of Hulan Design, a sustainable interior design firm in Orange California. What she sees on Southern California streets indicates most consumers aren't aware of their options for reducing this waste. "Neighborhood sidewalks on trash day hold a number of inexpensive furniture items," she says. "They're discarded by people who can afford to replace them with something new or of higher quality."

Hulan is an active participant in the local green design community committed to increasing awareness of sustainable design. She sees furniture rental as one solution for reducing this waste.

Reduces State Resource Usage

"Both resource and landfill management are affected by the discarding of short-term use furniture," says Hulan. Her projects over the past 16 years prove her deep sincerity when it comes to sustainable interior design. She has worked with Sundance Film Festival, the Teen Choice Awards, and LEED Platinum homes.

Hulan believes furniture rental could help reduce the number of state resources that are necessary to manage landfill waste. "In many circumstances, renting better quality furniture would be better for the environment rather than purchasing inexpensive 'throw away' furniture," she asserts.

Numbers supports that opinion. With pieces reused up to six times, rental furniture can produce up to 49 percent fewer greenhouse gases when compared to a direct sales model. For a state like California, that's compelling given initiatives like Under2 Coalition, an international pact among cities, states, and countries to limit the global average temperature increase to less than 2 degrees Celsius. Anything above that temperature could lead to catastrophic consequences.

Raises Recycling to the Next Level

Research has shown that individuals and elected officials want to see eco-friendly habit changes that increase sustainability. Even when consumers don't want to pay more for certain things, they often get behind initiatives designed to help the environment in a real way. In some cases, that could mean limiting the carbon footprint by raising recycling to the next level.

If your budget is tight, furniture rental allows you to furnish your home with more high-end furniture than you could afford to purchase outright. When you're done with the furniture, you simply return it. When you rent from CORT Furniture Rental, the furniture is refurbished for rental to another customer. If the furniture's rental life is over, 97 percent of it is discounted and resold to the public at a clearance center, extending its full life cycle even further.

This makes furniture rental the ultimate recycling program that could help with battling problems like climate change. "It is much better to return something for re-use by others than to discard it," says Hulan, who rents or borrows furniture for her events. "We all live on this little blue planet, and there are only so many places we can extract resources from and later throw them away."

3. HOW TO FIND ECO-FRIENDLY & SUSTAINABLE FURNITURE IN THE MODERN WORLD

Interest in sustainable furniture continues to grow as eco-friendly technology becomes a mainstay in our everyday lives.

How to Find Sustainable Furniture?

Finding sustainable furniture all begins with research. It's easy for companies to claim their furniture is green or eco-friendly, but many organizations now certify sustainable furniture materials. Educate yourself about these certifications and what qualifies furniture as sustainable, and you'll be able to make smart decisions regarding your furniture purchases.

What Are Sustainable Furniture Materials?

Sustainable furniture materials include a variety of resources, from reclaimed wood to LED lights. The type of material, as well as how it was obtained, factor into its sustainable classification. The Forest Stewardship Council (FSC), for example, certifies wood as sustainably harvested. Sustainable, responsible harvests ensure that the natural ecosystem remains in place and is able to maintain itself. As a result, the forest continues to grow and produce wood. Tree farms and forests are examples of areas that qualify for certification.

Recycled and Reclaimed Materials

Some eco-friendly furniture companies use reclaimed or recycled materials, like wood, glass and iron to create sustainable furniture. Old furniture, homes and other structures often provide the reclaimed items. Companies have even used factory wood scraps or flawed wood pieces for their sustainable furniture. Wood is a popular choice for manufacturers because it's durable, even if it's been mishandled throughout the years. Reclaimed pine, for example, is a popular finish for the Cristallo table.

The Rainforest Alliance helps determine if a piece of furniture actually uses reclaimed wood. The non-profit organization provide the Rediscovered Wood Certification to qualifying furniture pieces. Sustainable furniture may also be certified Cradle to Cradle (C2C), which in part says that the furniture can be dismantled. Its individual parts can be recycled at a facility or reused in other furniture. Easy furniture disassembly also allows for quick and easy repairs, which extend the life of the piece.

Furnishings consisting of recyclable materials, like most plastics or metals, help eco-friendly furniture companies by saving them from purchasing additional resources.

Non-Toxic Lacquers

The familiar "new car" smell associated with cars, furniture and other items is a result of manufacturers using unnatural and sometimes toxic substances, like solvent-based lacquers, to treat or finish a product. Solvent-based lacquers contribute to the pollution in your home by emitting, or off-gassing, volatile organic compounds (VOCs), like formaldehyde. Water-based lacquers are a green alternative to finishing wood furniture.

Furniture can be certified by Greenguard or Oeko-Tex for low toxicity rates. Unfinished furniture can also be found, though you'll still want to varnish it with natural wood finishes to extend its life and protect it from heat, moisture and general wear.

If you're unsure if a varnish is solvent or water-based, check the label. Most varnishes will note if they have a low VOC, which is what you want.

LED Lighting

LED lights are common in today's households because of their sustainability. They're far more energy efficient and have longer lifetimes than conventional light bulbs. In fact, LED light bulbs last 25 times longer and, in comparison to traditional light bulbs, use 90 percent less energy. Longer light bulbs help reduce waste and if adopted by everyone in the U.S., would power 2.5 million homes.

CARB2 Compliant

The California Air Resources Board (CARB) is behind the CARB2 compliance certification. CARB2 applies to hardwood plywood, particleboard, and medium-density fiberboard and indicates the material has the most minimal level of formaldehyde. Unsafe formaldehyde in homes can cause sore throats, asthma attacks and other symptoms, which is why it's important to, again, use water-based lacquers for preserving furniture.

In addition (and just as important), the CARB2 regulations prohibit the release of formaldehyde into the atmosphere during the production of composite wood products and their effect on global warming as well as the above-mentioned health issues.

Third Party Certifiers have been approved by the State of California to monitor this production and the labeling of the wood products as CARB2 compliant and these labels follow the wood products onto the furniture itself and the shipping documents, packing materials and into the retailers' possession and onto the final consumer.

Sustainable furniture made from composite wood, which is a mosaic of wood pieces glued together with a resin, will feature a CARB2 sticker if they're compliant.

Biodegradable Materials

Biodegradable furniture materials include plant products, wood and paper. Biodegradable materials are ideal for furniture that will inevitably wear out, like a mattress. Mattresses typically last five to 10 years and are often retired to landfills. Biodegradable mattresses ease the guilt with throwing out an item, as they'll decay and give back to the environment. Resource Furniture offers a full line of 100% non-toxic, biodegradable mattresses.

Understanding what qualifies as a sustainable material, as well as what certifications are available, makes it easier when you search for sustainable and eco-friendly furniture companies from which to purchase furniture.

What to Ask and How to Find Sustainable Furniture Companies

Of course, you might be wondering how to find an eco-friendly furniture store. You may not have many local brick and mortar options, depending on where you live. Luckily, you're guaranteed to find sustainable stores and products online.

The Sustainable Furniture Council (SFC) maintains a database of furniture manufacturers who are geared toward eco-friendly furniture and practices. But, because the SFC doesn't have strict standards, like requiring sustainable harvesting, some furniture stores listed aren't 100 percent sustainable or eco-friendly.

Talk to Showroom Employees

Employees at many eco-friendly furniture stores are knowledgeable and up-to-date on the latest trends in the industry. Talking with employees and asking them questions can help you discover if their company is truly offering sustainable products. Ask them about their company's sustainable practices, certifications and, most of all, about the furniture. Find out if it's easy to replace individual pieces, for example, or if the furniture has a non-toxic stain.

Showroom employees should easily know the answers to these questions. If they do not, take that as a sign that the pieces may not be as eco-friendly as you would hope.

Learn About Shipping

Also, consider researching the company's shipping practices. Eco-friendly companies focused on sustainable practices often strive to reduce their carbon imprint, which is one reason why sustainable furniture generally is able to be fully disassembled.

When disassembled, the furniture can be flat-packed for shipping. Unlike the transportation of assembled furniture, flat-packed furniture allows carriers to fill their trucks to capacity and prevent additional delivery trips and fuel stops.

Freight carriers, shippers, and their affiliates are also moving to more eco-friendly shipping methods. SmartWay Transport Partnership is a collaboration between the Environmental Protection Agency (EPA) and the transport industry to reduce emissions and boost energy efficiency.

Tactics, such as aerodynamic panels, speed limitations, and new exhaust systems have helped shippers reduce their emission rate. New technology has also helped by finding more efficient delivery routes.

So far, the partnership has saved the equivalent of powering 12 million homes in fuel, as well as reduced transportation's air pollution by 94 million tons.

More than 3,500 companies are a part of the SmartWay Transport Partnership. Don't hesitate to ask an eco-friendly furniture store if they're involved. It could encourage them to partner and ship with companies that are a part of the effort.

Why Living Small Is Sustainable

Downsizing is a great way to live in a more sustainable way. Smaller living spaces, whether a cozier home or a micro-apartment, use less energy, are easier to heat and have a smaller carbon footprint.

In the U.S., 53 percent of a home's energy use is linked to heating and cooling. Together, heating and cooling sources release more than 300 million tons of carbon dioxide each year. Add in offices and other buildings, and North America alone produces 2.2 billion tons of carbon dioxide every year.

A smaller living space is a viable way to minimize your impact on the environment. Many sustainable furniture stores design furniture specifically for smaller locations. Murphy beds, for example, have been stylishly redesigned into transforming sets for twin, queen and bunk beds that incorporate eco-friendly sofas or desks which allow a single space to function like two spaces or more.

Multi-purpose, space-saving furnishings go beyond eco-friendly bedroom furniture. Space-saving tables, nightstands and closets are also available to support a green lifestyle throughout your home.

Light, compact green furniture makes it easy to transition from a larger home or apartment to a smaller one. It also helps organize your life in whole new ways.

How Sustainable and Eco-Friendly Furniture Impacts Others

Outsourcing is a common topic of discussion when it comes to brand-name companies. It's public knowledge that many conglomerates outsource their manufacturing and pay their outsourced employees significantly less. More than 300,000 jobs are outsourced from the U.S. each year, with many companies citing decreased costs as their primary incentive.

Similar to asking eco-friendly furniture companies about their shipping, composition and design of their goods, it's important to look into a company's production and manufacturing practices and standards. Do they, for example, manufacture their furniture in a country that supports and follows the International Bill of Human Rights standard for equal pay for equal work?

It may seem trivial while you're browsing the internet to find sustainable furniture, but it relates directly to why you're looking for eco-friendly and sustainable furniture. You're thinking about your impact on the world.

Buying from eco-friendly furniture stores that pay all of their employees equally supports that company's commitment but also contributes to your personal impact on the world and everyone else in it.

Sustainable Furniture Means Quality & Durability over Low-Cost & Replaceable

Eco-friendly, sustainable furniture is designed to last. The goal is to conserve, not to contribute to the local landfill, after all. Sustainable furniture outlasts traditional furniture for a few reasons. First, sustainable furnishings are designed to be fixable. As noted earlier, most sustainable pieces are easy to dismantle. When your nightstand handle or chair leg breaks, it's a hassle-free fix because the furniture is easy to take apart and repair.

And it makes sense: We don't throw away our bicycles when they get a flat tire, we replace the tire and continue riding. Furniture qualifies for the same treatment.

Traditional furniture doesn't receive that treatment, however, which is why more than 9.8 million tons of furniture enters the landfill each year and, subsequently, why the furniture industry anticipated consumers to spend more than $106 billion dollars on new furniture in 2016.

While sustainable furnishings can break, like anything else, they're not necessarily easy to damage. Eco-friendly and sustainable furnishing companies manufacture their products with high-quality, durable materials. Again, the goal is to create a product built to last.

Lifetime or limited warranties demonstrate a company's commitment to their product. Resource Furniture's Clei wall beds, for example, include lifetime warranties.

Product sustainability extends beyond a product's framework, but also to its upholstery. While traditional upholstery may require professional cleaning, sustainable furniture often features upholstery that can be removed and cleaned or replaced.

Sustainable furniture outlasts traditional furniture because eco-friendly furniture stores understand their audience. Well-made furniture is a long-term investment that pays off because it doesn't have to be replaced again and again. If it did, it wouldn't be sustainable or eco-friendly.

Why Buying Vintage Furniture Is a Sustainable Option

Vintage furniture doesn't offer the same benefits as compact, multipurpose furniture, but it is a sustainable option. It can also complement your eco-friendly furniture and recreate what TV character Frasier Crane once described as an eclectic style of decorating.

Unlike present-day furniture, most vintage pieces were produced and manufactured without today's modern mass-production methods. Purchasing vintage furniture doesn't contribute to ongoing manufacturing and production methods, such as job-outsourcing or deforestation.

Due to its age, most of the toxic chemicals from the furniture will have dissipated, and you won't have to worry about off-gassing. Locally purchased second-hand furniture also reduces the environmental impact of transporting or shipping a bulky item to your home.

Purchasing older furniture eases a landfill's load and prevents a quality piece of furniture from being thrown away. Also, vintage furniture has resale value if you choose to sell it later.

4. 15 STRANGELY STYLISH SUSTAINABLE FURNITURE DESIGNS

From drinking straws to bicycle parts and airplane wings, who says your furniture has to be made of custom first-run materials? As sustainability becomes more a part of mainstream culture and the masses embrace the idea, eco-friendly furniture designers are getting more daring with creative materials and concepts. Sometimes that translates into stunning, stylish pieces that are easy to integrate into everyday life, and sometimes the results are a bit bizarre.

Self-Inflating Chair Dress

Not many people would consider the idea of walking around with a giant inflatable butt that wobbles up and down with each step you take, but artist Joo Youn Paek isn't deterred by embarrassment. Her 'Self-Inflating Chair Dress' is a wearable piece of furniture made of a pair of shoes, pumps and polyethelene. As demonstrated in the video above, when the wearer walks, air is pumped into the dress to blow up the derriere-area of the dress. The wearer can then sit comfortably – for about 10 seconds, until the dress deflates. Bizarre, but brilliant.

Flatpack Downloadable Furniture

Dutch designer Alexander Pelikan has designed some super-modern, flat pack furniture that you can build yourself by downloading the plans online. He hopes that downloadable furniture is the wave of the future, saying "The future could be fully digital furniture where the customer only buys the file needed for manufacture, steps to the closest milling facility and lets his piece be produced locally on the spot. And in this way 'immaterialized' product would cut down a lot on transport- and material costs, be very environmentally-conscious and above all it would broaden the freedom of design…"

Tables Made from Car Panels

The 'Elsie Series' by Nine Stories Furniture reclaims automotive sheet metal for reuse in furniture such as tables and shelves. Over 70% of each piece in the series is made from this otherwise wasted material. Nine Stories found that the automotive paneling worked great not just from a sustainability standpoint but from an aesthetic standpoint as well.

Bedside Table Turns into Bat and Shield

Worried about home security? The 'Safe Bedside Table' is designed to make you feel more secure. This two-in-one design transforms from a bedside table into a bat and shield so you can fend off invaders. Just throw your lamp out of the way, take it apart and start flailing away. It might work even better if the intruder sees you pulling the table apart to use it against him, just for the shock factor.

Airplane Wing Writing Desk

Nobody knows stylish recycled furniture like Reestore, the contemporary eco design firm behind the bathtub chaise, the shopping trolley chair, the wash drum table and the 'Deborah' airplane wing writing desk, pictured. Sleek and simple, this design takes the use of airplane parts as furniture out of the realm of novelty and into usability.

Magazines and Junk Mail Transformed

ReVision tables, created by teen artists apprenticing at Artists for Humanity in Boston, are meant as a response to the growing market need for innovative sustainable design. They're made from reclaimed junk mail and magazines, rolled up and stacked together in the form of tables which are then finished with non-VOC eco-friendly resin that makes them water-resistant and easy to clean.

Inflatable Garbage Chair

Don't toss those plastic bags and bottles into a recycling bin – you could be using them as furniture. The XS chair, designed by California College of Arts student Nick DeMarco, utilizes a clear plastic casing that holds discarded materials. It's not just an art project, though – DeMarco actually got a production deal with Wal-Mart, which will distribute it for $60 each.

Chairs from 100% Recycled Plastic Bottles

Cohda Design makes chairs out of 100% waste plastic. The chair is called 'RD4', with RD standing for 'roughly drawn'. How appropriate considering that the chair looks like a sketch come to life. The second photo, via Inhabitat, shows how the chair is made by winding the extruded plastic around a form.

Stylish Furniture Made from Bicycles

The collection of recycled bicycle furniture by Andy Gregg goes beyond the table previously featured on WebUrbanist – Bike Furniture Design takes old bicycles and breathes new life into them, resulting in gleaming chrome creations with a sleek, modern look. Some designs use additional recycled parts other than bicycles including automobile windows as tabletops and automotive seat belt webbing for seating upholstery.

Tennis Ball Benches

A steel frame and dozens of tennis balls makes for comfy seating at the Museum Boijmans Van Beuningen in Rotterdam. Dutch designers Tejo Remy and Rene VeenHuizen say the same qualities that make tennis balls bouncy make them perfect for cushioned, sturdy seating. Unfortunately, it seems as if brand new tennis balls were used for this project, but if the designers had teamed up with tennis players to use discarded balls no longer fit for playing, it would have been quite a smart ecological design.

Drinking Straw Furniture

Promise Design found an unexpected way to reuse thousands of drinking straws by stacking them together to create a chair and ottoman. The simple design doesn't involve much more than that, but it's certainly a creative way to prevent such items from ending up in the waste stream. In addition to the chair and stool, a lampshade and partition are available.

Recycled Human Hair Chair

Pounds and pounds of cut human hair is hauled to landfills from salons around the world every week. One designer realized the potential of this untapped renewable material and found a way to mix it with a matrix to produce a strong material that could be used as an alternative to fiberglass. The 'Stiletto Chair' by Ronald Thompson is made of 4.5 pounds of hair and though the bronze-coated prototype costs $15,000, Thompson is looking to develop less expensive models.

Human Nest Chair

The 'human nest chair' by Emily Pilloton is entirely constructed of cast-off scraps. Pilloton was inspired by the way birds use detritus for their nests and wanted to apply that concept to the human home. So she found a discarded papasan chair, built a base from scrap wood and scavenged bins behind a fashion design school for fabric. It took her six months and 40 yards' worth of fabric scraps to complete the chair.

Meander Transforming Ottoman

Is it a stool? An ottoman? A lounge chair? Basically, it's whatever you want it to be. The "Meander" by Talus Furniture uses polygonal shapes attached with zippers that can be manipulated to serve you however you need it to. Such a design could allow you to cut back on the amount of furniture you have to buy for your home. You could probably create some pretty fun Frankenfurniture with it, too.

'Perch' PVC and Copper Pipe Resting Spot

The 'Perch' chair by Rich, Brilliant, Willing doesn't exactly lend itself to cozying up with a book or relaxing after a rough day on your feet. It's more of a 'resting spot', and beyond that, a symbol for the need to view materials in a new way. Made of PVC and copper pipes, the $900 'Perch' could be a great seat for an artist working at an easel.

ABOUT THE AUTHOR

I am Phieby Ibrahim. I have been a university writing tutor and writing instructor for many years and loves researching, reading, writing, and discussing ideas. An admitted adrenaline junkie, he married his skydiving instructor and loves to go adventuring with him and their kids. I've compiled a great list here and I've excited they're all in the one spot. I hope you enjoy it as much as I enjoyed making it!

When you finish this book it would be amazing if you could leave a review for me as it'd mean the world.

Thanks so much for reading by my little corner.

Hope you enjoy the book!